HOOP-LA

Riddles about Basketball

by Rick and Ann Walton
pictures by Susan Slattery Burke

Lerner Publications Company · Minneapolis

To Peter Ivie, who's traveling —R.W. & A.W.

To my wonderful daughter, Perrin, for her inspiration in this first year of her life —S.S.B.

Copyright © 1993 by Lerner Publications Company

This book is available in two editions:
Library binding by Lerner Publications Company
Soft cover by First Avenue Editions
241 First Avenue North
Minneapolis, MN 55401

Library of Congress Cataloging-in-Publication Data

Walton, Rick.
   Hoop-la : riddles about basketball / by Rick & Ann Walton :
pictures by Susan Slattery Burke.
       p.   cm.
   Summary: A collection of riddles about basketball, such as "What
are a basketball player's favorite flowers? Guard-enias."
   ISBN 0-8225-2339-6 (lib. bdg.)
   ISBN 0-8225-9639-3 (pbk.)
   1. Riddles, Juvenile. 2. Basketball—Juvenile humor.
[1. Basketball—Wit and humor. 2. Riddles. 3. Jokes.] I. Walton,
Ann, 1963-   . II. Burke, Susan Slattery, ill. III. Title.
PN6371.5.W3544   1993
818'.5402—dc20   92-25771
                                                CIP
                                                AC

Manufactured in the United States of America

1 2 3 4 5 6 98 97 96 95 94 93

Q: What do basketball players do when they're happy?

A: Courtwheels.

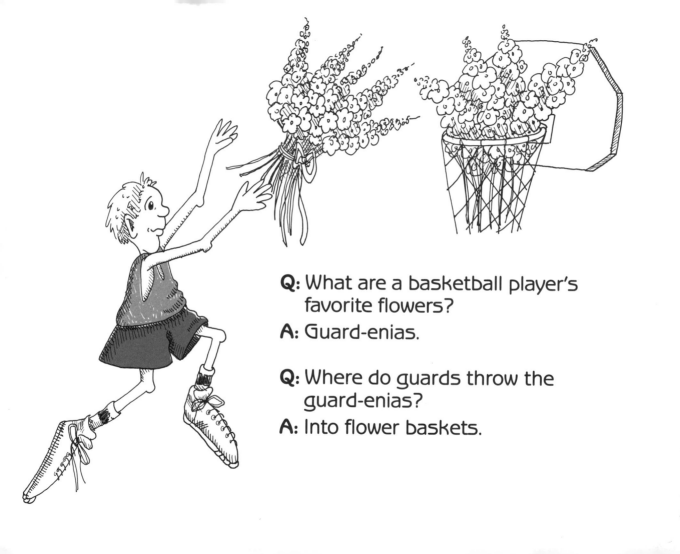

Q: What are a basketball player's favorite flowers?

A: Guard-enias.

Q: Where do guards throw the guard-enias?

A: Into flower baskets.

Q: Why do people like basketball players?
A: Because basketball players are court-eous.

Q: What sport do undertakers like to play?
A: Casketball.

Q: What sport do bakers like to play?
A: Biscuit ball.

Q: Why do happy ghosts play basketball?
A: Because they're high-spirited.

Q: What do you call an unbelievable story about a basketball player?
A: A tall tale.

Q: What do basketball players put on their sandwiches?

A: Ball-oney.

Q: What do basketball players snack on?

A: Turnovers.

Q: What do you get if you swallow a basketball hoop?

A: Hoopatitis.

Q: What do you get if a sick basketball player breathes on you?

A: Hooping cough.

Q: What do you get if you swallow a basketball?

A: A ballyache.

Q: When do basketball players go to the beach?

A: At high tide.

Q: Where do basketball players go sailing?

A: On the high seas.

Q: Why did the referee blow the whistle on Christopher Columbus?

A: Because he was traveling.

Q: What position did Abraham Lincoln play on his basketball team?

A: He was the cent-er.

Q: Where do centers grow?
A: In center fields.

Q: How do you catch the Atlanta Hawks?

A: In the New Jersey Nets.

Q: What kind of shots do the Hawks take?
A: Flew shots.

Q: Where do the Hawks like to stand?
A: At the fowl line.

Q: What do you call a sweaty basketball player?
A: A hot shot.

Q: What do you get if you drop an atomic bomb on a basketball court?
A: Nuclear foul out.

Q: Why do basketball players look at the shot clock?
A: To see how much time they've killed.

Q: What do you call a game between the Celtics and the Westside Elementary Fourth Grade All-Stars?

A: A Boston Massacre.

Q: Who roots for the players who sit on the bench?

A: The chair-leaders.

Q: What basketball team has good eyesight?

A: The L.A. Lookers.

Q: Which basketball players have nice lawns?

A: The L.A. Rakers.

Q: When soldiers play basketball, what happens when they lose?

A: They're court-martialed.

Q: Why was the basketball player arrested?

A: Because he stole a ball and shot a basket.

Q: Where was the arrested player taken?

A: To the basketball court.

Q: How did the police think the basketball player died?

A: They suspected foul play.

Q: Where did he go when he died?

A: To the Hoopy Hunting Ground.

Q: What team did the prince want to be on?

A: The Sacramento Kings.

Q: What are the Kings best at doing?

A: Holding court.

Q: What did the center do when he became a King?

A: He acted high and mighty.

Q: What should you call a basketball star?
A: Your highness.

Q: What do basketball stars sign autographs with?
A: Basketball-point pens.

Q: Where do rich basketball players keep their basketballs?
A: In ballrooms.

Q: What's seven feet tall, plays serious basketball, and pulls everything toward it?

A: The center of gravity.

Q: Why did the coach take away his players' credit cards?

A: To keep them from charging.

Q: Who brings presents to basketball players at Christmas?

A: Center Claus.

Q: How can you stop a basketball game?
A: Tear it from rim to rim.

Q: If a basketball court is torn from rim to rim, can it be fixed?
A: No, it's hoopless.

Q: If you want to play basketball on the ocean, what do you need?
A: A courtship.

Q: And who do you need on your team?
A: A coast guard.

Q: How do you get to the Phoenix Suns?

A: With the Houston Rockets.

Q: What basketball team specializes in driving to the basket?

A: The Milwaukee Buicks.

Q: What makes the Milwaukee Buicks run?

A: The Detroit Pistons.

Q: How fast was the basketball player running when she knocked over a player on the other team?

A: At foul speed.

Q: Why did the player take the basketball home?

A: Because the referee declared it a free ball.

Q: What did the referee call when one player threw another into the air?

A: A foul-up.

Q: What's gray, weighs 4,000 pounds, and loves to play basketball?

A: A hoopopotamus.

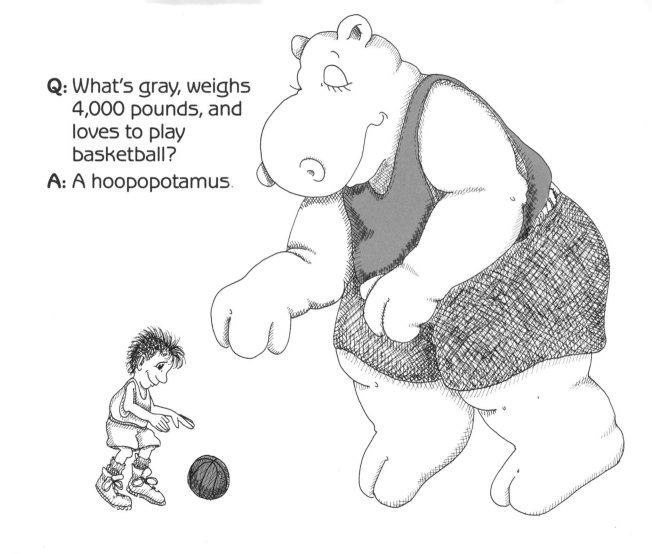

Q: How can a bad basketball player improve his game?

A: Through hoopnosis.

Q: Why do babies make good basketball players?

A: Because they dribble all over.

Q: What do you get if two babies play basketball together?

A: A double dribble.

Q: What do basketball players play when they're young?

A: Hoopscotch.

Q: Who's small and red and hangs on to the basket?

A: Little Red Riding Hoop.

Q: Who taught Cinderella to play basketball?

A: Cinderella's coach.

Q: What position did the skunk play on the basketball team?

A: Scent-er.

Q: Why is basketball such a quiet game?
A: Because the players wear sneakers.

Q: When are basketball courts flattest?
A: When they're run through a
full-court press.

Q: Why did the tired rabbit
have to give up the ball?
A: Because she was
out-of-bounds.

Q: What's the difference between a race downcourt and a bowl of oatmeal?

A: One is a fast break, the other is a breakfast.

Q: What do basketball players eat their oatmeal out of?

A: Basketbowls.

Q: What do basketball players watch on Saturday mornings?

A: Courtoons.

Q: What should you do if it starts to snow while you're playing basketball?

A: Play it cool.

Q: Why aren't trained dogs allowed on basketball courts?

A: Because they keep jumping through the hoops.

Q: Why did the basketball player throw the hoop in a lake?

A: Because she wanted to sink a basket.

Q: What do team owners pay at the end of the month?

A: Their basket-bills.

Q: If there were one second left in a game, and you threw the ball the length of the court trying to make a basket, would you make it?

A: Not by a long shot.

ABOUT THE AUTHORS

Rick and Ann Walton love to read, travel, play guitar, take walks, study foreign languages, and write for children. Rick also collects books and writes music, and Ann knits and does origami. They live in Provo, Utah, where Ann is a computer programmer and Rick is learning to weave baskets. They have two extraordinary children.

ABOUT THE ARTIST

Susan Slattery Burke loves to illustrate fun-loving characters, especially animals. To her, each of her characters has a personality all its own. She is most satisfied when the characters come to life for the reader as well. Susan lives in Minnetonka, Minnesota, with her husband, two daughters, and their dog and cat. Susan enjoys sculpting, reading, traveling, illustrating, and chasing her children around.

You Must Be Joking

Alphabatty: Riddles from A to Z
Help Wanted: Riddles about Jobs
Here's to Ewe: Riddles about Sheep
Hide and Shriek: Riddles about Ghosts and Goblins
Ho Ho Ho! Riddles about Santa Claus
Hoop-La: Riddles about Basketball
I Toad You So: Riddles about Frogs and Toads
Off Base: Riddles about Baseball
On with the Show: Show Me Riddles
Out on a Limb: Riddles about Trees and Plants
Take a Hike: Riddles about Football
That's for Shore: Riddles from the Beach
Weather or Not: Riddles for Rain and Shine
What's Gnu? Riddles from the Zoo
Wing It! Riddles about Birds